T0209241

I Didn't
KNOW
He Wanted More

LEEANNE CREECH

WESTBOW
PRESS®
A DIVISION OF THOMAS NELSON
& ZONDERVAN

WestBow Press books may be ordered through
booksellers or by contacting:

WestBow Press
A Division of Thomas Nelson & Zondervan
1663 Liberty Drive
Bloomington, IN 47403
www.westbowpress.com
1 (866) 928-1240

ISBN: 978-1-5127-9288-1 (sc)
ISBN: 978-1-5127-9287-4 (hc)
ISBN: 978-1-5127-9289-8 (e)

Library of Congress Control Number: 2017910276

Print information available on the last page.

WestBow Press rev. date: 07/03/2017

This book is dedicated to Orphan Relief and Rescue. They have lovingly gone into a dark and difficult country to become the hands and feet of Jesus. When I see the joy on the faces of so many children and adults who were previously without hope, it makes me tremendously happy. It would be easy for us to go about our lives and never confront the pain and suffering of these and so many other children around the world. Orphan Relief and Rescue daily faces the issue head on. Thank you!

Contents

Author's Note ix

Introduction xi

**Part 1 Three Early Events
That Shaped My Life**

Chapter 1   It Really Was a Dark and
            Stormy Night! 3

Chapter 2   Hell, Fire, and Brimstone! 7

Chapter 3   Missionary Night 11

Part 2 Off to Africa

Chapter 4   It All Started with the Cat.... 17

Chapter 5   Book Club 23

Chapter 6   Benin 29

Chapter 7   Elaine's Story 33

Chapter 8   Martin 39

Chapter 9   A Nighttime Visitor.............. 47

Chapter 10 Microfinance Program.......... 51

Chapter 11 Pencils!............................... 69

Chapter 12 The Big Boys 75
Chapter 13 The Sewing Girls 81
Chapter 14 Make a Joyful Noise............ 85
Chapter 15 New Wine 91

Author's Note

The names of the children have been changed to protect them from any danger. I have also avoided using specific locations as well as the names of the in-country staff and antitrafficking team.

Introduction

I've been a writer all my life. In my mind, I've started at least a hundred novels, mostly mysteries. My favorite plot line includes the long-lost "bad" twin who returns to cause all sorts of murder and mayhem. Of course I've never come close to completing any of them. Maybe I should say I'm a lifelong book starter. So you can understand my confusion when I heard God's gentle voice telling me to write a book. "What?" I was pretty sure I had heard incorrectly and chose to ignore the whole thing. But, of course, the little voice only got louder and more insistent. So off we go.

One of my favorite life-describing metaphors is a ball of yarn. You begin by wrapping yarn around a square piece of cardboard or other object that is not round. Gradually the pointy corners round out and the ball takes shape.

It gets bigger as new lengths of yarn are added and the knots are buried. Eventually, aha! A beautiful, soft, round ball of yarn.

That's where I felt I was in my life when God asked me to go to Africa.

Part 1

Three Early Events
That Shaped My Life

Chapter 1

It Really Was a Dark and Stormy Night!

I grew up in a typical all-American family, if there is such a thing: father, mother, two kids, dog, and a house in the suburbs. My dad went to work every morning in a suit: a white shirt, a tie, wing-tip shoes, and a felt hat, which was standard work attire for the 1950s. About once a month, he would get out his shoeshine kit and we would line up to shine, brush, polish, and buff!

Mom was the perfect homemaker. I have many happy childhood memories, but knowing she would be there when I got home gave me so much security and confidence, which I am only now understanding and appreciating.

As for my brother and me, our job was to go to school and be kids.

Brother Bill is eighteen months my elder, and growing up, we were pretty normal siblings. I idolized him and he ignored me, unless the neighborhood boys needed another person to even up the teams. As a result, I became quite good at sports and loved all things athletic.

Looking back, I think the greatest gift our dad bestowed on us was his deep and abiding love for our mother. We truly grew up believing that all families were like ours: happy parents, happy kids, all-American family.

The first life-changing event that I can remember happened in 1954. I was eight years old and don't remember having a care in the world. Our parents were out for the evening and we had a teenage boy from the neighborhood watching us. It was windy and rainy when they left, but soon the thunder and lightning began and the power went out. I was sitting in the window watching the light show when the babysitter walked up behind me and said, "You don't have to be afraid, little girl. God is always with you."

My immediate reaction was to fire back at him, "I'm not afraid!" After all, what self-respecting tomboy would be afraid of a little thunder and lightning? What I didn't say was that my whole body had gone a little tingly. It had something to do with God, but I was completely ignorant on the subject. I had heard the word *god* used in a sentence, but it had never affected me like this. We were not a churchgoing family, and I really knew nothing about Him.

My plan to find out about God was simple. Whenever I was alone, I would turn around as fast as I could, hoping to catch Him! It made sense at the time. After all, if He was busy always being with everyone, there would come a time when He was distracted and that would be my moment. Of course, I never caught Him, but not for lack of trying. I just wasn't quick enough! The real miracle was that I never doubted that He was there. Faith didn't come from me. It was a gift, given to me, that I would continue to learn about for the rest of my life.

Looking back on that night, I know my life changed forever just by hearing His name. I don't remember who that sitter was. I wish I did, because I would love to talk with him. He said one sentence to me, and it shook me to the core.

Don't ever discount a simple thing we may say to someone. God might use it for His good purpose.

Chapter 2

Hell, Fire, and Brimstone!

The next several years passed without much new "God" information. I asked my mom to take me to church, but she pretty much said no. "We're Methodist," she told me, "and there is no Methodist church in our town."

It was almost five years later before much progress was made. I was in junior high and introduced to a whole new group of friends. Jane was one of my best friends at the time, and one day she invited me to attend Sunday school with her family. I was so excited the night before that I could hardly sleep! Sunday school led to youth group, and I finally began to learn more about God.

Sunday became the best day of the week for me. I loved the singing and threw my whole self into it, despite having a voice only a mother could love. Those hymns and choruses remain very important to me.

One Sunday night in 1958, our youth group drove into Seattle to hear an evangelist speak. At the time, I didn't know what an evangelist was, but I was 100 percent into all things youth group!

I didn't really have any expectations for that night. I just remember being happy to be there and curious about what I would hear. After about three minutes, my eyes were as big as saucers! This man was yelling at us as he described the horrible pain of eternity in hell. He pounded his fist on the pulpit and described the flames that licked at us and never stopped. That was followed by a serene, safe, and glorious description of heaven. I was incredibly glad to hear there was an option! After that came a vivid reminder of the hell part, just in case we had forgotten.

By the time he had finished, I was totally confused! Oh, I knew where I wanted to end up. I just had no idea how to get there. He had been talking about Jesus, but nothing was connecting for me at that time. Jesus was the Christmas guy and nothing more.

When it came time for closing, he asked us to close our eyes and bow our heads. Next came a rehashing of the whole message followed by an invitation. Anyone who wanted to ask Jesus into his or her life and go to heaven should raise his or her hand. Mine shot straight up! He had asked us not to peek, which was an invitation to peek, so I did. I was literally dumbfounded to see only two other hands raised. *People*, I thought, *are you not listening? Why is not every hand raised? Do you all want to go to hell?* I was shocked. It never entered my mind that I was wrong to raise my hand, just that this whole room was very confused!

Those of us who raised our hands were asked to stay around to talk to a counselor. Let me say something here. Twelve-year-old tomboys don't want to sit around talking to little old ladies! Youth pastors are great, and our own youth group leaders would have been fine, but a little old lady? I don't think so! When she asked me if I understood what I had done, I said yes and left quickly.

I did understand one thing: Jesus was in my life, and I wasn't going to hell!

Chapter 3

Missionary Night

Over the next few months, the blanks began to fill in. Our church, youth group, and staff were amazing, and I am forever grateful for good early teaching. I was surrounded by wonderful adults who truly cared for us, and my life revolved around Sunday.

At school, I felt awkward and uncomfortable. It was more difficult for athletic girls to find their niche in the '50s. Youth group became a haven for me. I just loved being there. It was my safe place.

During the summer of 1958, we had a youth retreat weekend somewhere in a cabin in the Cascades. It was a first for me, and I was packed by Wednesday! No excitement here!

The theme of the weekend was the trial of Jesus, which we reenacted as if it were in a modern-day courtroom. It became clear that the evidence against Him was pretty flimsy, and I felt a terrible injustice had been done. Killing Him was so unfair. As the weekend progressed, I came to understand that He had to die. It was the first time I ever thought about my own sin and what it cost Him. He had to die for me.

One night that fall, our youth group gathered for a regular Sunday meeting. We had a missionary couple come to share about their work in Africa. The woman did all the talking, and this is what I remember from that evening: she was really old and frumpy! She had to be at least *fifty* years old and was wearing a plaid wool skirt and a green pullover sweater.

When she began speaking, I put my childish first impressions aside and hung on every word. On one hand, I was fascinated by the stories but also scared by her vivid descriptions. Someday, I wanted to share similar experiences, but in much nicer and safer places. By the time she finished, I believed God was calling me to missions. I know I was very young, but the feelings were overwhelming. When I went to bed that night, I prayed, "Dear God, if You want me to be a missionary, I will, but please don't make me wear skirts, and please, please don't ever send me to Africa!"

Part 2

Off to Africa

Chapter 4

It All Started with the Cat

More than fifty years have come and gone since those three events. I continue learning who God is. He continues to save me from hellfire and brimstone, and I'm not a missionary.

Many times, I have looked back and wondered what might have happened if I had followed His calling. I would always remind myself of the obstacles and buy into the white lie that we are all missionaries wherever God puts us. If I'm honest though, I regret not going a more direct route!

Now that I was seriously into the "senior citizen" set, I felt quite content with my life. I'd managed to navigate the bumps and bruises life throws all of us with my sanity intact. I had two amazing adult sons who love their mother, so I knew I'd done something right!

Yet if I looked back on my ball-of-yarn spiritual life, I was not so content. I thought God had been able to make a couple of potholders and maybe a pair of mittens with my life yarn, but I felt like I was just going through the Christian motions. I was kind of burned out on women's Bible studies, my prayer life was reduced to mostly saying grace, and I was getting used to God feeling very far from me. I figured I was okay though, because I suspected my Christian life was just like most churchgoing believers.

Many years ago, in a weak moment, I stopped by the local Humane Society and adopted a cat: Madam Olivia. She looked like an orange-and-vanilla sherbet cup and was generally good company. Olivia was a rescue kitty who had been abused by her previous owner and was delighted to move in with me. We had eleven good years together, but as she aged, her digestive system became our worst enemy! Every meal that went down returned after a short stay. Please trust me when I say I tried everything. The vet told me there was nothing wrong with her, but sometimes this happens to aging cats.

When I would be gone for a week, my wonderful neighbor would come over twice a day to feed and play with Olivia. Since cleaning up kitty barf was too much to ask anyone, you can imagine how things looked when I returned.

After a couple of years of this, I realized I was planning my life around when and for how long to leave Madam O. It came to a head when a very dear old friend was visiting. Jerry is my first youth pastor from those early days I described to you. Now in his eighties and battling Alzheimer's, I hugged him tightly as he was about to head home. He began to weep and said, "Please come and visit me." I said I'd try but immediately started to worry about the cat and how difficult it would be to leave her. I knew then that something had to change.

My friend Dana B. is some kind of animal whisperer! She knew Olivia well and wasn't surprised to hear from me when I was at the end of my rope. We agreed to go together with Olivia to the Humane Society. I could never bear to find out whether they found a miracle cure or she had to be put down. I only know I felt horribly guilty and expected many sleepless nights and lots of anxiety.

The very next day, I was driving by myself when I sensed the presence of God. He was saying to me, "It's okay. You did the right thing." His peace was so amazing! From then on, I haven't worried about Olivia, sleepless nights, or second-guessing.

Those special times in our lives when God seems so very near made me wonder why I didn't always feel that way. Was it possible He could be that close every day? I didn't think so. Many preachers over the years had talked about our faith being based in fact, not feelings, and that we need to be secure just knowing God is there because He said He would be, not because we are always intensely aware of Him. Nevertheless, I cherished those times when He was truly right there filling my heart and thoughts with the joy of His presence.

Chapter 5

Book Club

In the summer of 2014, the ladies in our church decided to have a monthly book club. The plan was to read a book and then meet together for discussion. Our first book was *Inspired to Action* by Rebecca Pratt. Rebecca and her husband, Tim, are the founders of Orphan Relief and Rescue (ORR), a ministry in Liberia and Benin, West Africa.

As I read the book, I was amazed at how this woman could see a need and be the conduit for making it happen. She was not afraid to face an insurmountable obstacle head on and watch God break down the barriers. I loved reading how hundreds of starving children were fed and how orphanages grew from seemingly nothing. At one point, Rebecca walked right into the office of a public official and left there with him on her side.

When I heard that Rebecca would be at our book club meeting to answer questions and share more deeply, I was excited! I was thinking that I might want to help ORR with a donation or perhaps volunteer at its headquarters. I was not thinking of going to Africa! In fact, I remember thanking God for these amazing people who do this work—and quietly being glad I wasn't one of them.

The meeting went well. We were able to ask lot of questions and learn much more about ORR and what has been happening since the book was published. It now had a successful microfinance program helping hundreds of village women in Benin. It was difficult to hear about the child trafficking in this poverty-stricken country, yet ORR was working increasingly in this area.

As I was driving home that night, my stomach began to feel funny and I knew I wasn't getting sick! God was getting my attention. It's not a long drive, and by the time I got home, I knew He was speaking to me. I did my best to ignore Him and try to convince myself He just wanted me to help support ORR, but by morning, it was very clear I would be going to Africa.

I remember praying that day, asking God if I was hearing correctly. Was He sure He wanted me to go to Africa? I reminded Him of my two least favorite things in life: flying and heat! His response was simple. He brought to my mind the night so very long ago when I begged Him not to ever send me to Africa. With tears rolling down my face, I knew in that moment He had flipped my heart completely around, and I was overcome with gratitude that He would give me this opportunity.

It would be a year and a half before the trip became reality, and during that time, I had a lot of work to do. *Do you know how many immunizations you need before going to West Africa?* I learned that if you rub your arm vigorously and wave it around for about five minutes afterward, it doesn't get sore. Of course, everyone who sees you thinks you're nuts, but I didn't care because it worked! I'm pretty sure I'm good to go for the next fifty years or so.

I don't think I've told you this yet, but I'm not exactly a tall person. In fact, if I really stretch, I can hit five feet. No one accuses me of being petite, so you can form a picture in your mind. I am sort of like a fire hydrant and not conducive to extremely hot weather. I didn't want to travel all that way only to spend my time sitting under a big tree and fanning myself. I wanted to be used in whatever way God had planned, and I knew I would have to get into better shape physically.

Not being an aerobics/Pilates kind of girl, at age sixty-nine I joined a CrossFit gym the last week of April 2015. I was by far the oldest in my group, and at first most people thought I would fade away when I found out how hard the workouts were. As time went on and I was still showing up, they became my biggest fans. If I looked like I might not make it, they would all rally around and cheer me on. After a long run, they would be waiting for me at the finish line, cheering as if I had won a marathon. Some would come back and run the remaining distance with me. I should say here that my son, Chris, was my biggest inspiration during this time. He had made major changes in his life due to CrossFit, and he would call me after every workout to tell me how proud he was of what I was doing.

Gradually the aches and pains lessened, and a few small muscles appeared!

We were scheduled to leave for Africa on March 1, 2016. After ten months of working out three days a week, I felt like I was in the best shape I could possibly be.

Chapter 6

Benin

Our team of five (Rebecca and four volunteers: Kathryn, Karen, Shannon, and I) left Seattle at 1:15 p.m. on Tuesday, March 1, 2016, and arrived in Cotonou, Benin, West Africa, on Wednesday evening. On a map, Benin is about one inch above the equator. It was hot!

Thursday morning, we headed up country to the orphanage safe house, our home for the next ten days. On the way, Rebecca briefed us on what to expect, how to stay safe, and what to eat and drink. Our well-nourished, generally healthy bodies could get in real trouble if we weren't careful. I knew Rebecca had been there several times and felt very comfortable following her lead. In other words, if she said something was okay to eat, it was okay to eat.

The trip was interesting to me, as it was hard to tell when we actually left the city limits. During the entire drive, the road was lined with people selling things. It would thin out a little, but there was never a time that felt like open spaces. At one point, we stopped to buy pineapples along the roadside. We never had to leave the vehicle but were surrounded by several women carrying large trays with pineapples on their heads. We purchased forty pineapples for ten cents each, and I must say I've never tasted such wonderful fruit. I also loved the way they cut the pineapples, so it was easy to eat with no waste.

Benin is considered a "dark" country in Africa because of the prevalence of voodoo, a religious practice where different "gods" are intertwined with every aspect of daily life. The city and villages that surround the orphanage safe house are considered the darkest in Benin. I knew this week would need to be bathed in prayer for every step we took, and I thought about my church and others who had promised to do just that.

Chapter 7
Elaine's Story

As we drove, Rebecca told us about Elaine. Elaine's parents had died when she was quite young and she was sent to live with her grandmother, who was the voodoo priestess for their village. Elaine had been forced into prostitution at age eight to earn her keep. She was also used in unspeakable voodoo sexual rituals and torture before coming to the orphanage safe house. We didn't really know her current age, but a good guess was fifteen or sixteen.

Rebecca told us that we would meet Elaine, but she probably wouldn't speak to us or join in on any activities. We would likely see her wandering around the orphanage grounds. She explained that Elaine's emotional growth had stopped around age eight but that she had a sweet temperament and we should just be kind when we saw her.

We arrived at the orphanage safe house about 2:00 p.m. Thursday afternoon and were immediately surrounded by beautiful, happy children who wanted to be hugged and loved by all of us. The first thing I learned was that they all spoke French, and I didn't. We did some "charade" communicating, but we also learned a few key phrases in French, mostly greetings: *Bonjour. Bonsoir. Comment ca va? Ca va bien.* Good morning. Good evening. How are you? I am fine. That is still the extent of my French vocabulary, but it was really all we needed.

Any time we would come walking out of our room, children would come running. They would hug us and we would say, *"Bonsoir, comment ca va?"* They would immediately smile and say, *"Ca va bien."* They would giggle and move aside for the next child to hug. They were sweet and gentle, and for the entire time we were there, we were never alone. If one of us sat on the couch for a short rest, in a matter of moments we would have as many snugglers as could fit! The adults who live at the orphanage safe house are wonderful people and dearly love and care for these little ones. There just aren't enough arms to continually hug them, so they were making the most of our time with them. Because of the Ebola epidemic, an ORR team had not been able to visit for over two years, which made them even happier to see us.

By Friday morning, I noticed Elaine standing off to the side while watching these hug fests. Friday afternoon, I turned to find her standing right next to me. I hugged her and repeated my French phrases, but she didn't respond and stood stiff just like a statue. After a quick prayer, I took her face in my hands and said, "Elaine, you are so beautiful, and God loves you so much." She smiled and walked away. The same thing happened about two hours later. She was still stiff and didn't speak, but she smiled and I was encouraged.

Later that evening, Elaine walked up to me and put her arms out for a hug. She really didn't wrap her arms around me, but she was welcoming as I went through the entire routine of speaking greetings in French and telling her how beautiful she was and so loved by God.

When I walked into the central hall Saturday morning, I saw Elaine standing across the room and looking right at me. I took a step toward her, and she responded by walking right into my arms. This time, after my French greeting, she replied, *"Ca va bien."* I tried not to react any differently. I just looked into her eyes and repeated what I had been telling her. "You are so beautiful, and God loves you so much." It was a wonderful moment, and my heart was breaking for this child who had suffered so much.

Walking into Sunday morning church service, I had no idea what to expect. The children had moved all the benches and were seated front to back, youngest to oldest. The older boys were playing drums, and many of the children were dancing joyfully and praising God. It made no difference that we couldn't understand the words; the meaning was beautiful and inspiring.

After the service, a member of our group asked the children if any of them would be willing to share how they felt about living in the orphanage safe house. Elaine stood up immediately! Our translator looked at us as if to say that Elaine was standing by mistake, that she didn't understand the question. We turned back to face Elaine, and the beaming smile on her face spoke volumes. She spoke clearly. "I like to live here because I know I am loved." We had only been there three days, but if I had gone home that day, it would have been with a full heart.

Chapter 8

Martin

Benin is a very poor country with a per capita income under three dollars per day. Because of this extreme poverty, many people are faced with selling their children in order to survive. This idea is completely appalling to us but has become a way of life for them.

Rebecca had talked to us about the antitrafficking work ORR was doing in Benin, but I didn't understand how that whole process worked. Now I was learning that the Benin equivalent of Child Protective Services had a high level of respect for our antitrafficking team and would contact us if they became aware of a child in danger. Our in-country team of four—two men and two women—has some of the most wonderful people I have ever met. All four love God deeply and have a compassionate heart for children.

Almost from the moment we arrived at the orphanage safe house on Thursday, Rebecca had been on the phone. That first night at dinner, she told us what was going on. The antitrafficking team had been alerted to a child in danger in a nearby village, and we were all going tomorrow to meet him and see the circumstances for ourselves. I was overwhelmed! Just think: here I am in Africa, and now I get the opportunity to visit a remote village and actually participate in a child rescue!

After breakfast on Friday, we all loaded into a van and drove about thirty minutes to the village. When we left the main road, the road changed to a bumpy, reddish, dusty dirt— and I didn't see anyone around. Somehow, I expected a remote African village to be more junglelike, but this was dry and desert looking with few trees. We walked single file on a path until we came to a clearing surrounded by huts made from blocks of dried mud. In the middle of the small clearing was a round area with a gazebo structure made from thin poles and a thatched roof. The children of the village brought enough benches for us to sit on and placed them just outside the gazebo, near enough to be shaded by the roof. I was grateful, as it was 101 degrees that day—our hottest so far.

It's difficult to describe what I was feeling as I watched people gather around us. Children and adults alike seemed to come from everywhere as if we were a giant magnet. I remember feeling very small yet part of a much bigger whole. As I prayed for what would unfold that day, two things became clear to me. First, it seemed as though God was very close. It was literally like talking to the person sitting next to me. Second, I knew in that moment that if God was not in the center of this ministry, of everything ORR was doing, that we would fail. We would be able to help feed and clothe the poor and needy, but unless there was a heart change, a transformation from within, nothing would last.

Through our antitrafficking team, which was also translating for us, the story began to unfold. Martin's mother had died, and he had been sent to live with his father in another village while his younger brother lived here with the grandmother. The grandmother told us that at his father's house, Martin had behaved badly and no one could control him. At the time, I wondered about this story because Martin and his brother were calmly sitting about two feet from me; he was quiet and still.

As Rebecca began to ask questions, the truth surfaced. We learned that Martin had been fine at his father's house, but his father didn't want to keep him. Grandmother finally admitted she had no natural affection for Martin. She loved his brother and wanted to keep him but just didn't want Martin. She was basically saying that if we didn't take him, he would either starve to death in the village or be sold into slavery. A choice like this was so far beyond my ability to understand that my mind didn't even try.

By this time, her husband arrived and explained that he had four wives and twenty children. He appeared to be an important person in the village, as people seemed to nod in agreement when he spoke. The village women standing behind me were emboldened by his presence and began to murmur that Martin needed to go. I found real anger welling up inside as I listened to these people giving this young life so little value. He was disposable to them. Basically, Martin was a five-year-old child on his own, surviving only because someone would give him a mouthful of food on occasion. Now all the village ladies were murmuring and nodding that it would be best if we took Martin with us.

While the husband was talking, the grandmother got up and went into her mud hut. She returned with a bowl of water and gave some to the brother, completely ignoring Martin. He never even looked at the water, as if he knew none would be offered him even though the temperature was over one hundred degrees. I wanted to scream but knew I couldn't. This was another situation where I trusted Rebecca was aware and I needed to be quiet and observe. It was excruciating for me to watch that small child with empty eyes.

Shortly after that, Rebecca turned to us with a glint in her eye. "Now I'm going to preach!" she said.

Through an interpreter, she explained God's plan for mothers and children. Careful to refer to God as the God who created them, she told them He created a special bond between mothers and children and that was a bond of love. She spoke for about fifteen minutes, and I noticed the village women standing behind me were crying. All the bravado was gone, as if they knew, deep inside it was wrong to turn their back on the children God had given them. Rebecca was speaking primarily to the husband, and he seemed to be getting smaller in the eyes of the villagers.

Every one of us wanted to grab Martin in our arms, hold him close, and take him immediately to safety, but I knew that wouldn't happen. We would need to talk and pray about the best way to handle this, but it was terribly difficult to leave him that day. It felt like we were abandoning him, but somehow it was the right thing to do. Patience has never been my strength!

Back at the orphanage safe house, Rebecca asked us what we thought about the whole situation. One by one, we agreed that something needed to happen quickly. Martin was in real danger. At that time, there were no beds available at the orphanage, but we all felt this couldn't wait. There would be a bed for him in July, but this was March. Without hesitation, one of our antitrafficking team said Martin could come and live with his family until a bed was available. Even though this man and his wife had three small children of their own in a tiny apartment, he was adamant. "We will take him." It reinforced to me that God had put the right people in the life of ORR.

That all happened on Friday, and a member of our team went to get Martin on Monday morning. The village women had bathed him and dressed him in new clothes, and we all saw him right after he left his village. He was a beautiful child, but his eyes were vacant. I can't imagine what he was thinking. Martin went home with our team member, and we saw him the next day. What a huge difference! He was much livelier, laughing, playing with the children, and willingly accepting the love being offered.

I am so humbled to have been a small part of this rescue. It's even difficult to write about it because my emotions come right to the surface. "Thank You, God, for letting me share in this amazing work You are doing."

Chapter 9

A Nighttime Visitor

I mentioned earlier that Benin is a dark country due to the voodoo worship and how talking about different spirits and believing in them is quite normal. This chapter is difficult to write, but I feel I must share even the uncomfortable things with you. Each day in this country had its challenges, wonders, and blessings, but our nighttime ritual felt like cool spring water to me.

We would arrive back to our room somewhere around 9:00 p.m., and my roommate, Shannon, and I would each take a shower. It's hard to imagine how wonderful that shower felt, considering the water was somewhere between chilly and tepid. The cool stream washed off the heat, sweat, and dust of the day and had an amazing ability to give us renewal. After showering, we had a chance to talk through the events of the day. Sometimes the conversation was light and easy, sometimes more difficult, but always there was laughter. The laughter really kept us going. Then we had a prayer time and went to sleep.

One night, I noticed Shannon having difficulty sleeping. I asked her if all was okay, but her answer was vague. In the middle of the night, she was up listening quietly to Christian music. Again, I said something, and again she told me everything was fine. I didn't believe her but didn't feel that pushing the subject was the right thing to do. The next morning, she seemed fine, so I didn't mention anything,

The following night, everything seemed normal, until the middle of the night when Shannon sat up and said, "Leeanne, pray for me; I'm being attacked!" In her voice was an urgency that was palpable. She was very upset, and I could actually feel the tension in her body.

I awoke immediately and held on to her as I began to pray. Without thinking, I began to pray, just as I had read in books for this situation. In Jesus's name, by the power of Jesus's blood, because of Jesus's death and resurrection, etc. I used the name of Jesus in every sentence and claimed the victory in His name. After about five minutes, she pulled back and said she felt much calmer and thought she could go back to sleep. Neither of us had much experience with demons, but we did know that Jesus had already won the battle and was the only name that could get rid of them.

I rolled onto my side in a semi fetal position and thought about what had just happened. Almost immediately, I was floating above my body while watching a black shadowy form completely surround me. I felt it physically and began to fight to free my arms, which were pinned up against my mouth. In those few seconds, I felt a physical terror and fought as hard as I could. When I got my arms free, I screamed, "Shannon!" But nothing happened, and I realized she couldn't hear me. So, I screamed, "Jesus, Jesus, Jesus!"

and the evil presence was immediately gone! The paralyzing fear was gone! In fact, I felt so calm I rolled over and went right back to sleep.

The next morning, we shared our experience with Rebecca, who told us she wanted to pray with us every night from then on. I learned later that our experience was not the first for volunteers or the ORR staff. Rebecca knew from past trips that these things sometimes returned, so we would have an extra prayer each night as a precaution.

They did not return.

Here is what I learned that night: Yelling for Shannon was a natural thing to do, but only the name of Jesus can have victory over such evil. Resting in His arms is where we are safe.

Chapter 10

Microfinance Program

On Tuesday morning, Rebecca ordered zimmies for us! "What's a zimmie?" I just know you are asking! A zimmie is a motorcycle, an African taxi if you will. They are less expensive than a van, and we would use them for any travel within ten miles of the orphanage safe house. They weren't the greatest-looking cycles I had ever seen. There was one that involved duct tape and chicken wire, but this was our mode of transportation, so we climbed on and off we went.

We would visit two villages that morning and meet many of the women on our microfinance program. This program began as an effort to stop the trafficking. If women were selling their children because they felt they had no other choice, then maybe we could provide them with a better option.

The plan was to loan them a small amount of money so they could start their own businesses and feed their families. If they paid back the initial loan, they could secure a larger amount to grow their businesses. Gradually, if all went well, they would have productive businesses and hope for the future.

The first village was quite small, and the ladies had gathered in a concrete structure maybe fifteen feet by fifteen feet. We were greeted with smiles and much excitement. Before long, they were singing and dancing around us, as if we were being honored. I had only been in Benin a short time, but I already loved the music, singing, dancing, and continuous clapping. I wanted to join in, but my American inhibitions and very bad dancing got the best of me.

Shortly after we arrived, the ladies performed a play they had written for us. It was a reenactment of the entire process of a child being sold into slavery with the promise of a better life for both the child and the family. The new owner promised to treat the child well and send the family money every year for their own support. The children, however, were not treated well. They were abused in every way possible. This little drama showed the village women talking to the mother, explaining to her about abuse and what had likely been going on with her child. Eventually, the mother began to weep and promised to never sell another child. I was unclear whether she was able to get her child back safely, but I did know she would if it was possible, and her remaining and future children would not have to fear being sold.

When I turned to Rebecca, she had tears running down her face. All she could say was "They get it!"

The two wonderful women on our antitrafficking team had been working with these ladies for a couple of years, and they were finally understanding that selling their children is not the right way. They realized

God has a beautiful plan for mothers and children. Children are a gift to be cherished and nurtured to adulthood. This is so difficult for them to grasp because in many cases they are not cherished by the men who impregnate them. Shortly after giving birth, they are pregnant again, and another child they cannot feed arrives.

I asked Rebecca about birth control, and she explained that most of these women have such a poor diet that their bodies can't handle any of the birth control methods we have available. For example, they do have birth control implants that are available, but they often can't be tolerated by their malnourished bodies, so it is a very poor solution to an ongoing problem.

The mood in the room was happy and hopeful. Because God had begun to change these women from within, they were becoming a community. They showed concern for each other and a willingness to help one another with children.

Rebecca shared a story with us about one of the villages where a little girl had been born, but her mother had died shortly after. When Rebecca first met this child, she was several months old but weighed less than ten pounds and was near death. She shared God's plan for mothers and children and admonished the village women to care for this child. Every time she returned, she would ask to see this little girl and encourage the surrogate mothers. Today this child is thriving, and a real sense of community has grown among the women of the village. It is wonderful to see the message getting through.

As we got ready to leave, they gave us a large bag of oranges as a thank-you gift. It was hard to receive from someone who had so little, but the look on their faces spoke such gratitude that we could not refuse.

After a short zimmie ride, we met the women of the second village outdoors. Again, there was much singing, dancing, and clapping. I loved the clapping and kept trying to catch on to the different rhythms, but they changed so often that I was lost.

Several of these women shared with us about the businesses they had started. Most made something to eat or cook with, or even clothing, and sold their wares in the market. Palm oil, soap, and baked goods were popular options. There were a couple of women who crocheted little hats, which many children were wearing. There was also a seamstress teaching some of the women to sew.

Currently, over 150 women are involved in the microfinance program. Of those women, at least one hundred of them had sold a minimum of one child in the past. To join the program, they are required to sign a contract agreeing to *never* sell another child and promise to raise them to adulthood. The women in our microfinance program take the contract very seriously, and to date we are not aware of any children sold by any of these women. In fact, the records show that 93 percent of the initial loans have been repaid and a larger loan has been given. Again, this speaks of a heart change among these beautiful women.

Riding back to the orphanage safe house, I thanked God for each one of these precious women and children. They live in such difficult circumstances, yet their lives express joy and praise to the God who created them.

We ate these delicious pineapples daily. They were beautifully prepared by the students in our culinary program at the orphanage.

The streets from Cotonou to the
orphanage were lined with vendors.

This precious girl at the orphanage safe
house wanted her picture taken!

These kids loved putting this puzzle together.

The author with several children
on the orphanage grounds.

Some of the happiest children in Benin
showing off their new dresses!

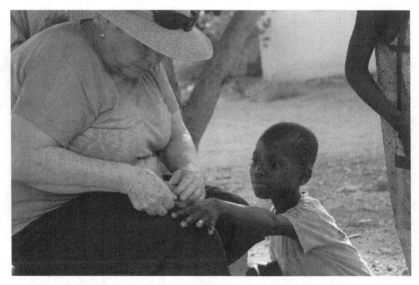

It's fingernail-painting day, and the
boys didn't want to be left out!

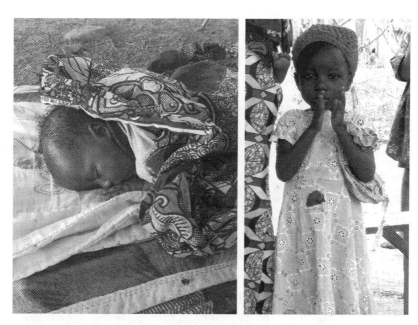

These two precious children live in remote villages.
Both of their mothers are in our
microfinance program.

Shannon with two boys on the
orphanage grounds.

Shannon had been coloring with these children.

Chapter 11

Pencils!

About a year before our trip, we each received a thick packet from ORR containing information about what to wear, immunizations needed, special items to bring, etc. The packet was formidable and more than I could handle at the time, so I skipped to a small section at the end, which listed things we could bring for the children: balloons, crayons, puzzles, clothing, pencils, fingernail polish, and so on. Not only was shopping for these things fun, but friends could easily add to our supply. When we all arrived at the orphanage safe house and laid out our goodies, it was amazing! Christmas in Benin! We had a little of everything and a lot of pencils!

Throughout the week, we had time to do some craft projects with the kids and used up many of our supplies. They especially liked coloring, and some worked hours on various art projects. No matter where you are in the world, kids and balloons seem to go together, and Africa is no exception. I tried multiple times to rub the balloon on my hair and make it stick to my blouse, but no luck. I was sure that would send them all into fits of laughter, but I guess the heat and humidity were not conducive to static electricity!

We were planning on a morning trip to visit a government school about thirty minutes away. In Benin, a child must supply his or her own uniform and box of supplies to be allowed in school. For many, this requirement is impossible, so they cannot attend. Sadly, children who cannot go to school are in even greater danger of being trafficked.

Orphan Relief and Rescue helps with a feeding program that directly impacts this school. People can support one of these children for thirty-five dollars per month, which provides the child daily with breakfast and lunch while at school. If we are able to rescue children from trafficking and provide two meals a day for them, they can live at home with their families, which is the best possible outcome.

We knew the school had about six hundred students, and we hoped we would have enough pencils to give one to each child. After putting aside enough for the orphanage kids, foster kids, and children of our antitrafficking team members, we carefully counted and had only 571! Shopping in the market yielded another twenty-five, but we left for school a few pencils short.

Before going into the classrooms, we met with the principal to get instructions from him and let him know of our plan. The first thing he said was there were 621 students! As we prayed, asking the Lord to provide enough pencils, it was hard not to think about Jesus feeding the five thousand!

We went to each classroom greeting happy children who were very excited to see visitors. In every room, they sang or danced for us, again with the rhythmic clapping I loved so much. We handed out a pencil to each child and received warm thanks. When we had gone completely through the school, we had so many pencils left over we gave them to teachers and helpers and still returned to the orphanage with pencils!

When the children were dismissed for lunch, we went outside with them. We were immediately surrounded by a large group of children who I noticed were not eating. Rebecca explained that while there were over six hundred students, only about one hundred fifty were on our feeding program, and another two hundred came from families who could afford the cost of the meals. This meant the remaining two hundred and fifty children were not fed. My heart was so grieved to hear this. It really hurt to watch some children walking around with bowls of food and still so many without.

For me, it was important to watch Rebecca at times like this. I knew her to be a loving and compassionate woman, yet she was able to handle this difficult situation without showing the righteous anger the rest of us felt. The need in Benin is overwhelming, yet Rebecca was slowly teaching me to rejoice in what was being done and never give in to the despair of what we couldn't do. As Christians, we are asked to care for others in Jesus's name, and maybe that's all we can do in some situations. Yes, it was hard to leave that school knowing many children were still hungry. On the other hand, it was a giant blessing for us to see 150 children safe from traffickers because ORR stepped in on their behalf.

Chapter 12

The Big Boys

At dinner, the first night we arrived in Benin, Rebecca told us we would see several different ministries where ORR was involved: the orphanage safe house, the microfinance program, the school-feeding program, and a sewing program in one of the villages where five girls, all rescued from slavery, were working to learn a trade to support their families. There were also two homes in the city that were fostering children who were not able to live at the orphanage safe house. These children were receiving tutoring to bring them up to their grade level so they could go to school. She explained that we would visit each of these places during our time here and asked us to let her know if God spoke to our hearts about a particular need. We would have some free time next week, and she would arrange for us to spend extra time wherever we felt led.

My first interest was the microfinance program. I believed so fully in the concept and thought I could help support that area when I returned home. But as our time there progressed, nothing really jumped out at me.

One afternoon, I walked into the large hall and sat down for a very brief rest. Immediately I was surrounded by several boys and again hampered by the language difference. I asked one of them how old he was, and he clapped once and put up two fingers. Twelve. As this seemed normal to them, I tried not to react and asked the next boy. He clapped once and put up one finger. Eleven. I loved it! I continued to marvel at how creative these people were. I enjoyed learning about every bit of their culture I could.

The next morning was the day we visited Martin in the village and learned that if we helped him, his only option was to go to a foster home, as there were no beds at the orphanage safe house. Rebecca explained that five of the oldest boys would be aging out in July and we would then have room for new children. In order for us to be in compliance with the local social welfare, we were not allowed to keep boys beyond the age of eighteen. I thought that must be so hard for them, to leave the only home they had ever known.

Rebecca told us ORR had rented an apartment for them across the street from the orphanage but that they would be on their own. "It's time to be men," she explained to them. I couldn't help thinking about my own boys and how difficult, and long, the process of moving out would be for these young men.

All of these things came together for me Sunday morning near the end of our church service. After the kids had a chance to share, they asked us to tell them something about ourselves. One by one, we went down the line and told our name, age, and a little about our families. As my friends were sharing, I remembered my time with the boys telling me their ages by clapping and decided that would be the best way to reveal my "advancing" age!

"Hello, my name is Leeanne, and I have two sons. Christopher is *clap, clap, clap, eight fingers!* And Brian is *clap, clap, clap, six fingers!*" The kids were all cheering, and I knew I'd have to continue. A quick glance at my friends, however, showed they didn't have the faintest idea what I was doing. "And I am *clap, clap, clap, clap*—rumble begins—*clap*—laughing and cheering—*clap, nine fingers.*" And the place went crazy! They were cheering and jumping up and down. I was caught between thinking "Wow, they've never seen anyone this old!" and "Hey, wait a minute. Sixty-nine isn't so old!" Their laughter and exuberance were contagious, and it was a perfect way to end the service.

As everyone began to mingle, I noticed all the big boys coming toward me. One by one, they knelt in front of me and took my hand, looked into my eyes, and said, "Grandmother." As they were showing respect for my age, I was so moved because my heart was full of love for them. I knew immediately that God was showing me where to spend any extra time, and I let Rebecca know right away.

A few days later, I had the privilege of spending time with these five boys and an interpreter. We talked about the move, their fears, and what the future held. I shared some things about my own sons' teenage years and tried to encourage them as much as possible. I promised to pray for each one of them every day and help in any way I could. Shannon had given me five quarters, and I gave one to each boy, telling them to remember their American grandmother would be praying for them and that I would try to help them in any way possible.

I smile when I get a text message from one of them. They start out, "Dear great mother of America." I think it's a translation thing, but I love it anyway! As I write this, their move is only two weeks away. Yesterday I asked one of the boys how they were all feeling, and he responded that they knew it would be okay because they knew God loved them.

I pray, "Dear Lord, surround these young men with Your love and strength, and watch over them."

Chapter 13

The Sewing Girls

One morning, we took a van to a village about thirty minutes away to visit the "sewing girls." These six girls ranged in age from around twelve to maybe eighteen. Age is often a complete guess in these villages. These children had been sold into slavery in Nigeria and had been there for differing amounts of time. Through the microfinance program, their mothers had been educated as to what really happened to their children and the possibility of getting some children back.

In many cases when a child is sold to traffickers, the families are promised an annual payment for the child, usually one hundred dollars. Of course, this money is never paid, but once the child is taken, most families have no recourse. If a family knows where their child is, and they have the means, they can get their child back by threatening to tell the authorities about the dishonest traffickers. The six girls in our sewing program were returned to their families with the promise that ORR would put them on a feeding program (the cost for one child is thirty-five dollars per month) and help them learn a trade.

These precious girls now live with their families but spend all day together learning how to sew. They have a room about ten feet square with six treadle sewing machines. Although the space is small and it is hot and stuffy, they are so very happy to be there!

Rebecca asked them questions to try to gently get them to tell their stories of captivity. One girl was in Nigeria for four years and learned to speak English quite well. She was working in a shop from morning until evening and was beaten daily. She was close to being sold again when ORR came and brought her home. She was so very thankful, and her smile confirmed that.

One of the girls was quite young, maybe eleven or twelve, and she described being in Nigeria for three years. She was working in the family business from 6:00 a.m. until 3:00 a.m. and then was allowed only three hours of sleep. I couldn't imagine anyone being able to keep this schedule for very long.

Each child had a difficult story to tell, yet they all felt ashamed of what had happened to them. Because of that, we had to read between the lines as to what else they may have endured.

One positive theme was constant. They were all so incredibly grateful for being rescued. They were not only learning to sew but they could also anticipate someday being able to support themselves. They had hope!

While we were there, the girls told us they wanted to make each of us a skirt. We walked through the village until we came to a woman selling fabric, and we each purchased some wonderful, colorful material. When we returned, the girls carefully measured each of us for our treasure. Their eyes sparkled with excitement, knowing they were doing something for us. It was a special time.

We returned a couple of days later and each modeled our skirt while the girls smiled, giggled, and pointed. We felt so blessed to see these girls free, safe, and happy.

Chapter 14

Make a Joyful Noise

Friday evening, Rebecca asked Shannon to give the message at church on Sunday and asked me to lead the singing. Little did she know. My lifelong lyrical road was a very bumpy one, but I'd never trade any of it. What I'm about to tell you is all true. No one could make this stuff up!

When I was eight years old, I tried out for the third-grade chorus. Thirty of us auditioned. We sang our little hearts out, and they selected twenty-nine. I remember pedaling my bike home with the tears running down my face. My mother didn't seem to think my rejection was such a great tragedy, so I bravely moved past my disappointment.

Fast-forward to age fifteen, when I was singing hymns in church with all the gusto I could muster. After four verses of "How Great Thou Art," the girl sitting next to me turned and said, "You are the worst singer I have ever heard." I learned to lip-sync and didn't make a sound in church for the next two years.

Fortunately, I grew up in the '60s and learned to play the guitar like most of my college friends. I'm not going to tell you I suddenly became a great singer—not even a good singer—but I did learn to stay on key if someone got me started off on the right note! This took a lot of concentration, because if I ever lost my place or my note, it was all over. What I'm saying is don't asked me to start "Happy Birthday"!

So, I smiled bravely and told Rebecca I would be delighted to lead singing at church. Gulp. The children loved to sing, and they already knew "Jesus Loves Me," so I planned to start with that one. We had been teaching them some songs during the week, and I wanted to stay within the safety of what they knew. Unfortunately, the choices were limited.

As I prayed about song choices, I was reminded of a chorus I loved as a young teen. It went, "Hallelu, hallelu, hallelu, hallelujah. Praise ye, the Lord!" The song involved standing and sitting as well as singing when you are supposed to—and singing loudly! I knew they would love it, but I was very unsure about the English/French problem as well as dividing the room into parts, etc. I wasn't sure they could say the word *hallelujah*, and worried about how confusing that might be for them.

Walking into church on Sunday morning, I was set on "Jesus Love Me" and "This Little Light of Mine" but was still unsettled on the third song. I didn't need to worry. The children were being led in prayer and at the end, they all shouted out, "Hallelujah!" Our amazing God is a God of details.

The children loved the song, and I don't remember ever hearing it sung with so much enthusiasm. What a huge blessing to walk around the orphanage safe house the rest of the week while hearing "Hallelu, hallelu" coming from the children's dormitory.

We were scheduled to leave the orphanage safe house on Friday morning around 10:00 a.m. to head back to Cotonou for a Friday night flight to Paris. I was certainly looking forward to getting out of the heat, sightseeing in Paris, and eventually sleeping in my own bed. On the other hand, I was struggling mightily with my own emotions, or should I say *lack* of emotions. I wasn't feeling anything. The other volunteers were weeping, hugging kids, and completely falling apart while I felt disconnected, like I was watching from a distance. I tried really hard to cry, squeezing my eyes together and thinking sad thoughts, but nothing worked. I honestly felt like a bad person, like I didn't care, but I knew inside, somewhere, that I did.

I closed my eyes and looked back on all I had seen over the past days. People everywhere were dying, starving, and surviving. People were enslaved, not only physically but also emotionally and spiritually. The orphanage safe house was filled with joy, giggles, and children being allowed to be children while knowing what they had been saved from. I thought of the women in the microfinance program, the girls sewing, the foster families, and the big boys. I remembered all the children who still needed our help, but we just didn't have the resources. Each time that happened, I'd try to concentrate on all the good we were able to do, but my heart ached for those we couldn't help.

What I realized in those few moments was that I was completely overwhelmed with all I had seen and done. I didn't feel anything, because I really didn't know where to start. It would be a process, and I would need to let it all unfold over the next weeks and months.

Chapter 15

New Wine

My mother died many years ago at a relatively young age, especially for someone so fit and healthy. She had a rare form of cancer and lived for eighteen months from the time of her diagnosis. During that experience, I learned something important about myself. I process things verbally. When something big comes along in my life, I need to talk about it, over and over. Often, it's the same conversation, the same questions with the same answers, but eventually things clarify for me. I will always be thankful for my cousin Dana M., who is an oncologist at the wonderful Seattle Children's Hospital. During Mom's illness, Dana received many calls from me and spent as much time as I needed talking and talking and talking. She knew I was asking the same things over and over, but she never made me feel like I was bothering her or intruding on her time.

For me, the post-Africa verbal processing began in Paris. I am thankful that Rebecca understood this about me because she began forcing me to think about circumstances I had experienced and talking to her about them. I remember walking through Notre Dame, a quick trip through the Louvre, and then the Metro ride to view the Eiffel Tower. All the time, I was talking about whatever came into my mind, endlessly. A couple of times, I thought Rebecca might show signs of verbal onslaught fatigue, but she was wonderful. Nothing really cleared up for me in Paris, but I had begun to put words to my thoughts and get things out.

Three days after arriving home, I cried for the first time. As I was sitting on the couch and praying for clarity, the tears came. This may sound naïve, but I wasn't expecting Africa to change me. The truth is a big part of me didn't want to change. I thought God asked me to go so I could be a part of helping those in greater need, perhaps to expand my horizons and see the world outside of my own comfort zone. Before my trip, I thought about all those things and knew they would be good for me. I was surprised to find out that those were just the beginning. There were still so many blanks to fill in, but I knew I would never be the same.

If you have read *The Voyage of the Dawn Treader* by C. S. Lewis, you will remember the scene where Aslan is peeling off the layers of dragon skin from Eustace. It's a fascinating description of how God deals with those of us who have never quite let Him have everything! Exposure is painful and difficult. Healing is wonderfully amazing! Over the next few weeks, I was on that journey, trying to understand what I had seen and done. I wanted to comprehend why God had taken me halfway around the world.

Every day after returning home, I felt His presence more deeply. During my nearly sixty years of living as a Christian, I could remember the times I felt Him this intensely. They are sometimes called mountaintop experiences, and I had probably had a dozen or so. I had always been taught these were special times He gives us to encourage us and keep us running the race. I was also told that I should take care not to put much store in feelings but to concentrate on studying the Bible, praying, and fellowshipping. This is all good, but I am a very black-and-white person. I took this to mean I could never expect to live every day on the mountaintop. Well, guess what? The top of the mountain is exactly where He wants us to live!

Six weeks after returning home, I was praying and feeling overwhelmed by His presence. My prayer was like this: "Lord, will You be with me like this always?" It was hard to even say, because I had never believed it possible. His answer was immediate and wiped away years of struggle to be replaced with His peace.

I think it's important here to say that I only did one thing. I said yes when He asked me to go. I didn't know He wanted more. In fact, I'm pretty sure that if He had said, "I want you to go to Africa, and when you get home I'm going to turn your world upside down and nothing will ever be the same," I would have run the other way. I'm very glad I didn't run.

I'm going to end this by sharing a poem God gave me during a very dark time of my life. I was in an emotionally abusive marriage and tried to protect myself by withdrawing into a bubble of sorts. Nothing got in or out, so nothing could hurt me anymore. After a few weeks, my complete lack of feeling scared me, and I cried out for help. In about ten minutes, this poem was written, and today, it means more to me than ever before.

In His Arms
I saw a picture yesterday,
like none I'd seen before.
You were seated on Your throne,
and I was on the floor.

I could see my human strength
just didn't mean a thing,
as I sat helpless looking up
before the Holy King.

I could see that all the things
I knew I'd done alone

held no meaning when compared
to the glory I was shown.

You are God, Almighty God,
Eternal, Holy One.
Then I could see and understand
that I was Your dear son.

You gently showed me through this scene;
I felt helpless and alone.
And then You picked me up, dear Lord,
and held me on Your throne.

I felt so small and frail, God,
enveloped in Your love,
Until You filled my emptiness
with Your descending dove.

The song that's in my heart today
is something very new.
I want to speak and shout and sing.
Holy Father, I love You.

I didn't know He wanted more. I didn't know
that the simple act of obedience would bring
so much more than I could ask or imagine.
I didn't realize going to Africa was as much,
if not more, for Him to work in my life. You

might say I was stubborn and thickheaded! If God had to take me all the way to Africa to make a point, then I am forever grateful that He did! What an amazing God who loves us always and forever, who is so longsuffering to wait while we fumble our way through this life. He never gives up on His children. He will never give up on you!

I titled this book *I Didn't Know He Wanted More*. Now I think what I meant was I wasn't ready to change anything in my life to find out. I was very comfortable in my daily walk: safe and secure, no big problems, nothing to ruffle my feathers. I was coasting, and I liked it. What I'm learning is this: not only does He want more of us, but He also wants to give us more—tremendously more—than we could imagine. I don't see that I've changed anything, but He has changed everything. Every moment of every day is a new adventure of discovery.

Many years ago, I had the privilege of meeting Irene Webster Smith, a missionary to Japan for most of her life. Beloved by the Japanese people, they called her Sensei (Teacher).

When asked about her life and work, she simply said, "As I go step by step, He will open up the way before me." I would like to be able to say the same thing as I walk this path daily.

If God is asking you to step out and obey Him in some way, please say yes.

If you are interested in knowing more about Orphan Relief and Rescue or helping to support its ministry, you can find information at www.orphanreliefandrescue.org.

The author can be reached at lcreech320@gmail.com.

Printed in the United States
By Bookmasters